What's red, white and crawls up your walls?

A baby with forks sticking out of its eyes.

_____

Why doesn't Mexico have an Olympic team?

Because everyone who can jump, run, or swim is already in America.

_____

How do you circumcise a guy from Alabama?

Kick his sister in the jaw.

_____

Why do Japanese sumo wrestlers shave their legs?

So they won't be mistaken for lesbians.

_____

Why do farts smell?

So deaf people can enjoy them too.

_____

What's the difference between a lawyer and a catfish?

One's a bottom-feeding scum sucker. The other's just a fish.

BOOK YOUR PLACE ON OUR WEBSITE AND MAKE THE READING CONNECTION!

We've created a customized website just for our very special readers, where you can get the inside scoop on everything that's going on with Zebra, Pinnacle and Kensington books.

When you come online, you'll have the exciting opportunity to:

- View covers of upcoming books
- Read sample chapters
- Learn about our future publishing schedule (listed by publication month *and author*)
- Find out when your favorite authors will be visiting a city near you
- Search for and order backlist books from our online catalog
- Check out author bios and background information
- Send e-mail to your favorite authors
- Meet the Kensington staff online
- Join us in weekly chats with authors, readers and other guests
- Get writing guidelines
- AND MUCH MORE!

**Visit our website at
http://www.zebrabooks.com**

HILARIOUSLY GROSS JOKES

Volume XXIX

Julius Alvin

Zebra Books
Kensington Publishing Corp.

http://www.zebrabooks.com

ZEBRA BOOKS are published by

Kensington Publishing Corp.
850 Third Avenue
New York, NY 10022

Zebra and the Z logo Reg. U.S. Pat. & TM Off.

First Printing: August, 1999
10 9 8 7 6 5 4 3 2 1

Printed in the United States of America

Contents

For Nick Santa Maria—

"Well, I didn't know . . ."

In A Word, Gross

So every time he traveled to New York City, the salesman always stayed at the same hotel, because the bellboy always managed to fix him up with the best hookers in town.

The salesman checks in. Unfortunately, the bellboy forgot that the salesman was arriving, and all the hookers are across town and busy. The bellboy runs out and buys a rubber blowup doll, hoping the salesman will be drunk enough not to know the difference.

Sure enough, the salesman rolls in at midnight, drunk as a skunk. The bellboy helps him up to the room and puts him to bed next to the rubber blowup doll.

The next morning, the salesman comes down and hands the bellboy the usual $100 tip.

The bellboy asks, "Was the company to your liking, sir?"

The salesman responds, "Son, that was the weirdest girl I've ever been with."

"How so?" the bellboy asks.

"Well," the salesman says, "I took off all my clothes. Then I rolled over on top of her. Then I gave her neck a little bitty bite."

"What happened then?" the bellboy asks.

The salesman says, "Damn girl farted and flew out the window."

What's the definition of a "sadist"?

A proctologist who keeps his thermometer in the freezer.

Why is the Catholic church finally going to let priests get married?

So they'll know what hell is really like.

———————

Why are black women such good dish-washers?

Their Brillo pad is built right in.

———————

What do you get when you cross a black woman with a Chinese woman?

Someone who'll suck your shirts.

Hear about the blind skunk?

He had a ten-minute conversation with a fart.

_____

How do you know when you're a bad driver?

You cut someone off on the expressway and your wife dies in the cross fire.

_____

How do you know when a Polish woman is having her period?

She's only wearing one sock.

How do you know when your girlfriend is really fat?

She sits on your face and you can't hear the stereo.

What do you call a black man in handcuffs?

Trustworthy.

Why are men like blenders?

Women need them, but they're not sure why.

This guy comes home one night, completely drunk. He's met at the front door by his wife, who is not at all happy.

"Where the hell have you been all night?" she wants to know.

"At this great new bar," her husband claims. "The Golden Saloon. Everything there is golden. It's got huge golden doors, a golden floor—the works. Even the urinal is gold!"

His wife is skeptical. She calls information and asks for a place called the Golden Saloon. Sure enough, the joint's listed. She calls up the place to check up on her husband's story.

"Is this the Golden Saloon?" she asks the bartender who answers the phone.

"Sure is," says the bartender.

"Does your establishment have huge golden doors?" she asks.

"Sure do," says the bartender.

"Have you got golden floors?"

"Sure do."

"And do you have a golden urinal?" she asks.

There's a pause, and the woman hears the bartender yell out, "Hey, Charlie—I think I got a lead on that guy who pissed in your saxophone last night."

What's red, white, and silver and walks into walls?

A baby with forks sticking out of its eyes.

Why don't sharks eat lawyers?

Professional courtesy.

How does a man know when his wife is cheating on him?

He buys a used car and finds her dress in the backseat.

Morris's wife of forty years passes away. The undertaker asks him, "Do you want her buried, embalmed, or cremated?"

Morris responds, "Why take chances? Do all three."

———————

What's the difference between a French poodle and a pit bull humping your leg?

You let the pit bull finish.

———————

Why do men lie to their wives?

Because the wives keep asking them questions.

A farmer from Arkansas walks into a lawyer's office to file for a divorce. The lawyer asks him, "May I help you?"

The farmer says, "Yeah, I want to get me a day-vorce."

The lawyer asks, "Do you have any grounds?"

"About a hundred acres," the farmer says.

"You don't understand," the lawyer says. "What I mean is, do you have a case?"

The farmer says, "I ain't no Case. I got me a John Deere."

"No," the lawyer says. "I mean, do you have a grudge?"

"Sure I got a grudge," the farmer replies. "That's where I keep my John Deere."

The lawyer says, "No, sir. What I need to know is, do you have a suit?"

"Sure, I do," the farmer says. "Wear it to church every Sunday."

Exasperated, the lawyer asks the farmer, "Look, does your wife beat you up?"

"Nope," the farmer says. "We both get up at 4:30 in the mornin'."

About to give up, the lawyer finally asks, "Let me put it this way: Why do you want a divorce?"

The farmer says, "Well, I guess it's 'cause we never seem to have a meaningful conversation."

Murray is dreading his fiftieth birthday. His best friend, Sam, says, "I know it sounds old, but don't worry. Remember: Life begins at fifty."

"Yeah," Murray says, "but everything else starts to wear out, fall out, or spread out."

———————

What are the three signs of old age?

The first is loss of memory. The other two we forget.

———————

What's the definition of "middle age"?

When it starts taking longer to rest than to get tired.

What's another definition of "middle age"?

When work is a lot less fun—and fun is a lot more work.

——————

What's the best way to live forever?

Live modestly, get lots of sleep, and lie about your age.

——————

What's the difference between a rectal thermometer and an oral thermometer?

The taste.

What's the difference between "ooooohhh!" and "aaahhhhh!"?

About two inches.

———————

The blonde says to her friend, "My boyfriend has the worst dandruff."

Her friend says, "Have you given him Head and Shoulders?"

The blonde thinks for a minute and replies, "No. How do you give shoulders?"

———————

What do you get when you play New Age music backward?

New Age music.

So this kid from Alabama goes into a drugstore and asks the druggist for a box of condoms.

The druggist says, "How old are you, son?"

The kid replies, "Eleven."

"I can't sell you any condoms," the druggist says. "You're too young."

The kid says, "Gimme some rubbers or I'll call a cop!"

"All right, cool it," the druggist says to the kid. "What kind of condoms do you want?"

The kid tells him, "Gimme the French ticklers."

The druggist says, "Listen, kid. Do you know what one of those things will do to a woman?"

"No," the kid replies, "but I hear they make a sheep jump that high!"

How many female country singers does it take to sing the song "Crazy"?

All of them.

_____

What do you call a turtle with a hard-on?

A slowpoke.

_____

What's the difference between a tick and a lawyer?

A tick falls off you when you die.

YOU KNOW YOU'RE DRINKING TOO
MUCH COFFEE WHEN . . .

1) Juan Valdez names his mule after
you.

2) You chew on your wife's finger-
nails.

3) You can jump-start your car without cables.

4) You do twenty miles on your tread-
mill before you realize it's not plugged
in.

5) You can't remember your second
cup.

6) You have a picture of your coffee
mug *on* your coffee mug.

7) Starbucks has a mortgage on your
house.

8) Your birthday is a national holiday
in Brazil.

9) You don't sweat—you percolate.

10) You grind coffee beans in your
mouth.

Gross Celebrity
Jokes

What were the last words Dodi Fayed said to his chauffeur?

"I said I wanted to fuck Di in the tunnel, not fucking die in the tunnel."

—————————

What did the Queen of England get Fergie for Christmas?

A Mercedes and a trip to Paris.

How do you get a Deadhead off your door-step?

Pay for the pizza.

———————

What does Kenny G say when he gets into an elevator?

"Wow! This place rocks!"

———————

How many lawyers does it take to pave a driveway?

About ten, if you smooth them out right.

What's the difference between a guitar player and a mutual fund?

A mutual fund will eventually mature and start making money.

––––––––––

What's the difference between an accordian player and brain surgery?

You get an anesthetic for brain surgery.

––––––––––

How many female country singers does it take to screw in a light bulb?

One. She holds the light bulb and the world revolves around her.

What killed Jerry Garcia?

Acid indigestion.

————————

What's a Tupac Shakur cocktail?

Five shots and you're dead.

————————

What's the toughest part of making love to Oprah Winfrey?

Setting up the on ramps.

Why does Stevie Wonder smile all the time?

He doesn't know he's black.

———————

What does Micheal Jackson hate about having sex?

Getting the bubble gum off his dick.

———————

What's the best thing about living next door to a Hare Krishna?

You get a free ride to the airport.

What's the definition of "saturated fat"?

Oprah in a hot tub.

———————

What do you call a Deadhead who just broke up with his girlfriend?

Homeless.

———————

How do you know when a Deadhead just robbed your house?

Your thongs are missing.

How did Michael Kennedy count down to New Year's?

"10-9-8-7-6-5-4-treee!"

_____

What was Michael Kennedy's New Year's resolution?

Eat more fiber.

_____

What was the last thing to go through Michael Kennedy's mind before he died?

A branch.

How do they know Michael Kennedy was
drunk when he died?

He got smashed on the slopes.

—————————

Why are Michael Kennedy and Christmas
alike?

They both give you a present under a tree.

—————————

What did Teddy Kennedy say when he
heard his nephew, Michael Kennedy, had
died?

"Who was driving?"

What's Michael Jackson's favorite TV show?

The Baby-sitters Club.

———————

What's the difference between Michael Kennedy and English nanny Louise Woodward?

Kennedy's baby-sitter was shaken by his death.

———————

What's Johnny Cochran's theory of law?

"A man is innocent until proven broke."

What do Cher and a pine tree have in common?

They were both nailed by Sonny Bono.

———————

Why did Sonny Bono die in a ski accident?

After being a mayor and a congressman, he wanted to be a Kennedy.

———————

What did Satan say to the Grim Reaper?

"I said Yoko Ono, not Sonny Bono!"

What came before Sonny Bono's senseless death?

Sonny Bono's senseless life.

———————

How was Sonny Bono's body found?

Sonny side up.

———————

What did Michael Kennedy say to Sonny Bono just before he hit the tree?

"Go out for the long one!"

What's the difference between Sonny Bono and Michael Kennedy?

About five days.

———————

Hear about Hillary Clinton's new book?

It Takes A Village . . . To Keep My Husband Satisfied.

———————

What's the difference between Bill Clinton and a gigolo?

A gigolo can only screw one person at a time.

What does Ted Kennedy have that Bill Clinton wishes he had?

A dead girlfriend.

What game did Bill Clinton play with Monica Lewinsky?

Swallow the Leader.

Why did Bill Clinton go out to sea on an aircraft carrier?

To promote offshore drilling.

Why is Bill Clinton interested in the Middle East?

He heard that the Gaza Strip is a topless bar.

———————

What does Ted Kennedy have that Bill Clinton doesn't?

A dead girlfriend.

———————

What did Ted Kennedy say to Bill Clinton?

"Why didn't you just drown the bitch?"

What's the difference between President Clinton and the *Titanic*?

Only 500 women went down on the *Titanic*.

What does Bill Clinton say to Hillary after he has sex?

"I'll be home in twenty minutes."

What's President Clinton's definition of "safe sex"?

When Hillary is out of town.

Why did President Clinton have a hard time firing Monica Lewinsky?

He couldn't give her the pink slip without asking her to try it on first.

———————

How does Bill Clinton keep Monica Lewinsky away from the White House?

He sends Ted Kennedy over to give her a ride home.

———————

What did Bill Clinton tell Congress about the new Abortion Bill?

"Go ahead and pay it."

How did Bill Clinton paralyze Hillary from the waist down?

He married her.

───────────

Why is President Clinton like a snowstorm?

Because you don't know when he's coming or how many inches you'll get.

───────────

What's the definition of a "virgin in the White House"?

A girl who can run faster than the President.

What do Monica Lewinsky and Bob Dole have in common?

They were both upset when Bill finished first.

———————

The Pope goes to Cuba to meet with Fidel Castro. The news media from all over the world go to Cuba to report on the historic event. A day later, though, all the reporters and TV newspeople split and go back to Washington, D.C.

Castro says to the Pope, "What happened to Dan Rather? Why did all the newspeople leave Cuba?"

The Pope replies, "Well, it seems that President Clinton got caught having sex with one of his interns."

Castro asks, "What exactly is an intern?"

The Pope replies, "It's something like an altar boy."

How did Bill and Hillary first meet?

They were both dating the same woman.

What did Bill Clinton say to Monica Lewinsky when the scandal hit?

"I didn't say lie in the deposition. I said lie in that position."

Why does Bill Clinton cheat on Hillary?

So he can be on top.

Why won't President Clinton ever be indicted?

Because Monica Lewinsky swallowed the evidence.

What did Monica Lewinsky's friends buy her for her birthday?

Kneepads.

What are the five shortest books ever written?

1. *My Plan To Find the Real Killers* by O.J. Simpson

2. *Mike Tyson's Guide to Dating Etiquette*

3. *To All the Men I've Loved Before* by Ellen DeGeneres

4. *George Foreman's Big Book of Baby Names*

5. *Al Gore: The Wild Years*

———————

What's THE shortest book ever written?

The Book of Virtues by Bill Clinton

So President Clinton goes out jogging one morning. He passes by a prostitute and asks her, "How much?"

The prostitute calls back, "Fifty bucks."

"I'll give you ten," Clinton says to her.

"No way," the hooker replies.

The next day he jogs by the prostitute again and calls out, "How much?"

"Fifty bucks," she tells him.

"I'll give you ten," Clinton says, and the prostitute turns him down.

The next morning, Bill goes out jogging with Hillary. They jog past the prostitute, who calls out to Bill, "See what you get for ten dollars?"

Now That's Sick!

What do you call it when a man talks dirty to a woman?

Sexual harassment.

_____

What do you call it when a woman talks dirty to a man?

$3.99 a minute.

What's the difference between a girlfriend and a wife?

Thirty pounds.

———————

What's the difference between a boyfriend and a husband?

Forty-five minutes.

———————

What's the definition of "making love"?

Something a woman does while the guy is fucking her.

How do we know that God is a man?

Because if God was a woman, sperm would taste like chocolate.

_____

Why didn't the man talk to his wife for eighteen months?

He didn't want to interrupt her.

_____

What would you do if your wife AND your lawyer were drowning?

Have lunch and take in a movie.

What do a gynecologist and a pizza delivery boy have in common?

They can both smell it but they can't eat it.

———————

How is a woman like a condom?

They both spend more time in your wallet than on your dick.

———————

What do a woman and Kentucky Fried Chicken have in common?

By the time you're finished with the breasts, all you have left is a greasy box to pop your bone in.

Why are tornadoes and marriage alike?

They both start with a lot of blowing and sucking, but in the end you always lose your house.

———————

Why doesn't Mexico have an Olympic team?

Because everyone who can jump, run, or swim is already in America.

———————

What do you call a dog with four-inch legs and six-inch steel balls?

Sparky.

How do you circumcise a guy from Alabama?

Kick his sister in the jaw.

———————

Did you hear that they discovered a new use for sheep in Wyoming?

Wool.

———————

What's a blonde's favorite nursery rhyme?

"Humpme Dumpme."

So the Polack comes home from work early and finds his wife naked on the bed, panting for breath.

"Honey," she says to her husband. "I think I'm having a heart attack!"

Rushing to call 911, the Polack almost stumbles on his four-year-old son. The kid says, "Daddy, there's a naked man in the closet."

The Polack throws open the closet door and sees his best friend standing there, naked as a jaybird.

The Polack says, "Damn it, Harry. My wife's having a heart attack and all you can do is stand there scaring the hell out of the kids!"

What was the smartest thing to ever come out of a woman's mouth?

Albert Einstein.

———————

How can you tell when your wife is dead?

The sex is the same, but the dishes pile up in the sink.

So this rich lady decides to throw a big birthday party for her daughter. She goes all out—having the whole thing catered, hiring a band and even a professional clown.

Just before the party starts, two homeless guys show up, looking for a handout. Feeling sorry for them, the woman offers them a meal, *if* they chop some wood for her out back.

The guests arrive, and the kids are having a great time. The clown calls to say he's stuck in traffic and won't be able to make it.

The woman is disappointed until she sees one of the homeless guys doing cartwheels all over the backyard. Then she watches in awe as he swings from tree branches and does a flip in midair.

Impressed, she says to the other homeless guy, "Your friend is fantastic! You think he would repeat that performance for my daughter's party? I'll pay you fifty dollars."

"I dunno. Let me ask him," the second homeless guy says. He calls to his friend, "Hey, Willie? Wanna chop off another toe for fifty bucks?"

What are the best ten things about being a guy?

1. Monday Nite football.

2. The lines to the bathroom are always shorter.

3. Your old friends don't care if you've gained weight.

4. Your ass is never a factor in job interviews.

5. All your orgasms are real.

6. Guys in hockey masks don't attack you.

7. You can go to the bathroom without a support group.

8. You can leave a motel bed unmade.

9. You never have to clean the toilet.

10. You can write your own name in the snow.

What did one black lesbian say to the other black lesbian?

"You the man!"

What's the difference between a man and a woman?

To a man, foreplay is optional.

What's another difference between a man and a woman?

Princess Di's death was just another obituary.

What's one more difference between a man and a woman?

If something mechanical doesn't work, you can bash it with a hammer.

Gross Racial Jokes

How many Los Angeles cops does it take to push a black man down a flight of stairs?

None. He fell.

_____

Hear about the Polish guy who bought a toilet brush?

A month later, he went back to using paper.

How come there's no Disney World in New Guinea?

Nobody is tall enough to go on the rides.

———————

Why do so many black people move to Detroit?

Because they heard there were no jobs there.

So this guy goes to a whorehouse in Chinatown. After haggling over the price, the Chinese hooker takes the guy upstairs to her room. She says to him, "So what's your pleasure?"

The guy says, "I want sixty-nine."

The Chinese hooker responds, "You want beef with broccoli now?"

—————————

Why didn't the U.S. Postal Service put Louis Farrakhan on a stamp?

Because people wouldn't know which side to spit on.

How do you make a Jewish girl scream twice?

Fuck her up the ass; then wipe your cock on her curtains.

————————

What did the Polish girl say to her husband when she got horny?

"Send the kids outside to p-l-a-y so we can go fuck."

————————

What's the difference between a rabbi and a priest?

One cuts it off and the other sucks it off.

What do you call a Mexican with half a brain?

Gifted.

What were Sam Houston's last words at the Alamo?

"Where did all those Mexican landscapers come from?

What happened to the black guy and the Puerto Rican when they jumped off the Empire State Building?

The black guy splattered on the street. The Puerto Rican got lost.

Why did the Polish lady get an abortion?

She didn't know if the baby was hers.

———————

Two black guys meet on the street. The first one says, "Yo, man, did you hear about Tyrone? He died."

"Shit," the other black guy says. "I didn't even know he got arrested!"

———————

What did the Polish girl do when she dropped her bubble gum in the toilet?

She chewed the shit out of it.

Did you hear about the Jewish Santa Claus?

He comes down the chimney on Christmas Eve and says, "Ho ho ho! Anybody wanna buy some toys?"

———————

What's the most popular booth at a Mexican carnival?

"Guess Your Age—One Dollar."

———————

What do you call six black women in a hot tub?

Gorillas in the mist.

What are the Ten Commandments in Ebonics?

1. I be God. Don't be dissin' me.

2. Don't be makin' hood ornaments outta me or nuthin' in my crib.

3. Don't be callin' me for no reason—homey don't play that.

4. Y'all best be in church on Sundee.

5. Don' dis yo mama, and even if you know who yo daddy is, don't be dissin' him neither.

6. Don't be icin' yo bros.

7. Stay wif yo own woman.

8. Don't be liftin' no goods, homey.

9. Don't be snitchin' on yo homeys.

10. Don't be eyein' yo homey's crib, muthafucka.

What's brown and has holes in it?

Swiss shit.

———————

Why did the Italians lose World War II?

They ordered lasagna instead of shells.

So the Jewish girl comes home and says to her mother, "Mom, I just married an Arab sheik!"

"You married an Arab?" her mother asks, shocked.

"It's okay, Mom," the daughter says. "He's worth billions of dollars. You and Daddy will live in luxury for the rest of your lives!"

The Jewish girl comes back from her honeymoon. Her mother asks her, "So how did it go?"

"He's an animal," the daughter says. "All he did for two weeks was boink me up the ass. The day we got married, my asshole was the size of a dime. Now it's the size of a silver dollar."

Her mother says, "So for ninety cents you're complaining?"

Gross Lawyer Jokes

What do you call a lawyer with an I.Q. of 50?

Your Honor.

_____

What do you call a corrupt lawyer?

Senator.

What's the difference between a lawyer and a trampoline?

You take off your shoes to jump on a trampoline.

———————

What do you call 5,000 lawyers lying at the bottom of the ocean?

A good start.

———————

How can you tell when a lawyer is lying?

His lips are moving.

How many lawyers does it take to roof a house?

Depends on how thin you slice them.

———————

How do you stop a lawyer from drowning?

Shoot him before he hits the water.

———————

How many lawyers does it take to stop a runaway bus?

Not enough.

What's brown and black and looks good on a lawyer?

A Doberman.

———————

What's the difference between a lawyer and a vampire?

A vampire only sucks your blood at night.

———————

Where do you find a really good lawyer?

In a cemetery.

What do lawyers use for contraceptives?

Their personalities.

Hear about the terrorist who hijacked a plane full of lawyers?

He threatened to release one every hour if his demands weren't being met.

What do you buy a friend who just graduated from law school?

A lobotomy.

What's the difference between a lawyer and a catfish?

One is a bottom-feeding scum sucker. The other's just a fish.

———————

What's the ideal weight for a lawyer?

About three pounds, including the urn.

———————

Santa Claus, the Tooth Fairy, an honest lawyer, and a drunk are walking down the street together when they all spot a hundred dollar bill on the street. Who gets it?

The drunk, because the other three are mythical creatures.

Gross Sex Jokes

So two little kids—one a six-year-old boy, the other a five-year-old girl—are outside playing.

The little boy says to her, "I'd really like to get in your pants."

"Is it because you think I'm cute?" the girl asks.

"No," the boy replies. "It's because I just shit in mine."

Two guys are drinking in a bar.

The first guy says, "I fucked my girlfriend up the ass last night."

The second guy replies, "No shit?"

"Well, maybe a little."

———————

Why is a pussy like a grapefruit?

They both squirt when you eat them.

A rabbi and a minister are seated next to each other on a plane. The stewardess comes up to them and asks, "Would either of you care for a cocktail?"

The rabbi says to her, "I'll have a Manhattan."

"Yes, sir," she says. "And you, Reverend."

"Young lady," the minister replies, "before I touch strong drink, I'd just as soon commit adultery."

The rabbi pipes up, "Lady, as long as we got a choice, I'll have what he's having."

What's the definition of the "perfect one-night stand"?

"GET OUT!"

_____

What's the most successful pickup line in Alabama?

"Baaaaaaaaaa!"

_____

How does a guy know when he has a high sperm count?

His girlfriend chews before she swallows.

What do you call a female turtle?

A clitortoise.

_____

When the surgeon came to see his young patient on the day after her operation, he found her slightly embarrassed.

"What's wrong?" the doctor asks her.

"Well," she says, "this is a little difficult for me to ask, but . . . how long will it be before I can resume my normal sex life?"

"I'm not sure," the doctor stammers. "You're the first patient to ever ask me that after a tonsillectomy."

Three guys go out to a strip club. Trying to impress his friends, the first guy pulls out a ten spot and beckons over one of the nude dancers.

"Watch this," the first guy says and sticks the ten between the dancer's tits.

"That's nothing," the second guy says. Then he whips out a fifty and sticks it in her twat. "Let's see you top that."

The third guy shrugs. "All right," he says. He takes out his ATM card.

"Whaddaya gonna do with that?" the first guy asks.

The third guy swipes the card between the dancer's butt cheeks, takes the sixty dollars, and goes home.

So the elderly couple are celebrating their sixtieth wedding anniversary.

"You know, Murray," the wife says. "I think we should go upstairs and make love."

The husband replies, "I'm sorry, honey, but I can't do both."

————————

What's the difference between a penis and a paycheck?

You don't have to beg your wife to blow your paycheck.

What did the stockbroker's wife say when her husband caught her cheating on him?

"Sorry, dear, but I've gone public."

_____

Why did the midget get kicked out of the nudist colony?

He kept getting in everyone's hair.

_____

What's the true definition of "sex"?

It's the most beautiful, natural, and wholesome thing money can buy.

Hear about the flasher who was going to retire?

He decided to stick it out another year.

———————————

A guy says to his girlfriend, "Do you know the difference between a conversation and making love?"
The girl replies, "No."
"Then lie down," the guy says. "I wanna talk to you."

———————————

How does a homosexual fake an orgasm?

He throws warm yogurt on his lover's back.

So the newlywed couple are strict Baptists and uptight about sex. They decide to call his penis "washing." Her pussy was referred to as "the washing machine."

One night, the husband cuddles up to his wife and says, "Honey, can I put my washing in your machine?"

"Not now," the wife says. "I'm too tired."

A little later, she's feeling amorous, so she says to her husband, "Okay, dear. You can put the washing in now if you want."

"No thanks," her husband says. "I just did the load by hand."

Why do Japanese sumo wrestlers shave their legs?

So they won't be mistaken for lesbians.

So the Irish girl comes home and says to her mother, "Mom, I have V.D."

"Put it in the cellar," her mother replies. "Your old man will drink anything."

What do Diet Pepsi and pussy have in common?

They both have a really bad aftertaste.

Why did the feminist cross the road?

To suck my fucking dick!

Why are women like toilet seats?

Without the hole in the middle, neither are worth shit.

———————

What happened when the woman fingered herself during her period?

She got caught red-handed.

———————

What's the difference between sperm and mayonnaise?

Mayonnaise doesn't hit the back of a girls throat at thirty miles an hour.

What does eighty-year-old pussy taste like?

Depends.

_____

What's the difference between a golf ball and a woman's G-spot?

A man will spend twenty minutes looking for a golf ball.

A Polish guy is arrested for walking around Grand Central Station stark naked.

"I know you're not going to believe this," the Polack says to the cop, "but I just got into town. I went up to this whorehouse with five of my friends. The madam tells the hookers to undress and stand against the wall. Then she told me and my friends to get undressed and stand against the other wall."

"Then what happened?" the cop wants to know.

"Well," the Polack says, "the madam told me and my friends to go to town, and I'm the first one here."

Why can't a man look a woman directly in the eye?

Because tits don't have eyes.

———————————

What did Bill Clinton like about Monica Lewinsky?

She had the prettiest smile he ever came across.

So the rich guy comes home drunk and attacks his wife. The police arrive and find the woman dead on the living room floor with a golf club next to her body.

"Is this your wife?" a cop asks the husband.

"Yes," the husband replies.

"Did you kill her?"

"Yes," the husband admits.

"It looks like you nailed her ten times with this three iron. Is that correct?"

"Yes," the husband says. "But could you put me down for five?"

———————

Why is PMS called PMS?

Because Mad Cow Diseases was already taken.

How do you know when a girl really likes you?

You stick your hand down her pants and it feels like you're feeding a horse.

———————

What do men consider safe sex?

A padded headboard.

———————

Why did the woman cross the road?

Who gives a shit. Why ain't she in the kitchen making dinner?

So the woman was despondent over not having sex in months and months. In hopes of finding a solution to her problem, she decided to see a doctor.

Going through the Yellow Pages, she came upon a Chinese sex therapist—Dr. Ching. When the woman arrived for her appointment, she told the doctor her symptoms.

Dr. Ching tells her, "Take off all your crothes and you craw real fass away from me across the foor."

The woman finds this request a little odd, but does it anyway, stripping naked and crawling from one side of the room to the other.

The doctor shakes his head and tells her, "You have real bad case of Zachary Disease—worse I ever see. Thass why you have sex ploblem."

"What exactly is Zachary Disease?" the woman wants to know.

The doctor replies, "Zachary Disease— when your face look zachary rike your ass."

Why do bald men cut holes in their pants pockets?

So they can run their fingers through their hair.

––––––––––

A Polish guy is performing oral sex on his girlfriend. He says to her, "You're really dry tonight."

She says, "That's because you're licking the carpet."

––––––––––

How do you embarrass an archaeologist?

Give him a used tampon and ask which period it came from.

A Truly Gross
Variety

What's the difference between love, true love, and showing off?

Spitting, swallowing, and gargling.

_____

What's the difference between Courtney Love and Wayne Gretzky?

Gretzky takes a shower after three periods.

What did the cannibal do after he dumped his girlfriend?

Wiped his ass.

———————

What's the difference between a bitch and a whore?

A whore sleeps with everyone at the party. A bitch sleeps with everybody at the party except you.

———————

Did you hear that Lorena Bobbit died in a car crash?

Some dick cut her off.

Why does Dr Pepper come in a bottle?

His wife died.

———————————

What's the difference between pussy and Mom's apple pie?

You can eat your Mom's apple pie.

———————————

What is blond, has six legs, and roams Michael Jackson's dreams every night?

Hanson.

Why is pubic hair like parsley?

You push it aside before you start eating.

———————

What's the difference between oral sex and anal sex?

Oral sex makes your day. Anal sex makes your hole weak.

———————

What's a lesbian's favorite flavor of ice cream?

Sardine.

What do you call a prostitute with a runny nose?

Full.

————————

How can you tell when you're at a bulimic bachelor party?

The cake jumps out of the girl.

————————

How do you make five pounds of fat look good?

Put a nipple on it.

What did Ellen Degeneres say to Kathy Gifford?

"Can I be Frank with you?"

———————

What are the three best movies to rent during a Jewish holiday?

1. *Shalom Alone*
2. *Who Framed Roger Rabbi?*
3. *A Gefilte Fish Called Wanda*

A man comes home from work early one day and finds the family doctor in bed with his wife.

"What the hell is going on?" the man demands.

"It's the strangest thing, but your wife has music playing in her chest!"

The husband goes over and listens to his wife's chest. He says, "I don't hear anything."

The doctor responds, "Of course not. You're not plugged in!"

A guy goes into a pet store and asks the owner for an unusual pet to keep his wife company while he's away on business.

The store owner shows him a parrot that costs a thousand dollars. The husband asks, "Why a thousand dollars for a parrot?"

"Because this isn't just any parrot," the owner says. "You like pop, the bird sings Sinatra. You like rock, it sings the Rolling Stones. You like opera, it sings Pavarotti."

The guy is skeptical. "I don't know. How come it's only got one leg?"

The store owner says, "Whaddaya want—a singer or a dancer?"

What did Yasir Arafat say to Bill Clinton?

"Sheep don't talk."

A trucker drives his fully loaded rig to the top of a steep hill. He's just starting down the hill when he sees a man and woman in the middle of the road fucking their brains out. He slams on his brakes and comes to a screeching halt only inches away from the naked couple.

The trucker jumps out and screams at them, "Are you crazy? Didn't you hear me blowing the horn? I coulda killed you."

The man replies, "Look. I was coming, she was coming, and you were coming— but you were the only one with brakes."

How do you find a fat girl's snatch?

You flip through the folds until you smell shit, then go back one.

———————

The Polack is fucking his wife in the ass for the first time. The wife cries out, "Ouch, that hurts!"

The Polack says, "No, it doesn't. It feels great!"

———————

A guy goes to San Francisco for the first time. He gets on the bus and sees that it's filled with gay guys.

The guy says to the bus driver, "I wanna get off."

The bus driver says, "Don't worry—you will."

Why do Italian women spend so much time at the beauty parlor?

The estimate alone takes three hours.

———————

What did the nun do when she got tired of using candles?

She called in an electrician.

———————

How can you tell the redneck at Sea World?

He's the one carrying the fishing pole.

Why do black women wear spiked heels?

To keep their knuckles from dragging on the sidewalk.

———————

What's the definition of an "optimist"?

An accordian player with a beeper.

———————

What do a priest and a Christmas tree have in common?

The balls are just for show.

A guy walks into a drugstore and asks the girl behind the counter for a package of condoms.

"What size?" she asks.

The guy doesn't know. The girl says, "Okay. I'll measure you."

She takes out a ruler, measures the guy's dick, and calls out, "Size large in aisle three!"

Another guy comes in and asks for a package of condoms. "What size?" the girl asks. The guy doesn't know, so she measures him too, then calls out, "Size medium in aisle two!"

A fifteen-year-old boy comes in and sheepishly asks for a package of condoms. "What size?" the girl asks.

"Uh ... I ... I don't, uh ... I don't know," the kid says, embarrassed.

The girl starts measuring his cock, then gets a really disgusted look on her face. She yells out, "Cleanup in aisle one!"

So one night, the farmer gets drunk. He grabs his wife's tits and says, "If these could give milk, we could get rid of the cows."

He grabs her butt and says, "If this could give eggs, we could get rid of the chickens."

The wife grabs the farmer's dick and says, "And if this stayed hard, we could get rid of your brother."

A preacher was telling his congregation that anything they could think of, no matter what, was discussed somewhere in the Bible.

One woman says, "Preacher, I don't think the Bible mentions anything about PMS."

The preacher thinks for a minute, then says, "Yes, it does. 'And Mary rode Joseph's ass all the way to Bethlehem.'"

What did Jesus say to Mary after he was nailed to the cross?

"Can you get me my flats? These spikes are killing me!"

———————

Why did the Japanese leper commit suicide?

Because he lost face.

———————

What's the best thing about a blow job?

The five minutes of silence.

A businessman is checking into his hotel when he accidentally jabs his elbow into the breast of a very attractive young lady.

He says to her, "Excuse me, madam. If your heart is as soft as your breast, I'm sure you'll forgive me."

The lady replies, "And if your cock is as hard as your elbow, I'm in room 312."

———————

Why did the Polish girl stand in front of a mirror with her eyes closed?

So she could see what she looked like asleep.

Two nuns are ordered to paint a room in the convent, and the last instructions from the Mother Superior were that they must not get even a single drop on their habits.

After conferring about this for a few minutes, the two nuns decide to lock the door of the room, strip off their habits, and paint in the nude.

In the middle of their painting, there's a knock on the door. "Who is it?" asks one of the nuns.

"Blind man," replies a voice from the other side of the door. The two nuns decide that no harm can come from letting a blind man in, so they open the door.

The man comes in and says, "Nice tits, sisters. Now where do you want these blinds?"

———————

Why should women wear Tampax when skydiving?

So they don't whistle on the way down.

What is the surest sign that a man is truly in love?

He divorces his wife.

———————

One day, a priest has been in the confessional too long and needs to take a leak. It being Sunday, the line for the confessional is really long, so he asks the janitor to fill in for him.

"But I don't know what to say," the janitor protests.

"Look, you've been to confession," the priest says. "There's a list of sins and penances taped inside the booth."

The priest leaves and the janitor hears the first sinner.

"Bless me, Father, for I have sinned," says the voice, which the janitor recognizes as one of the altar boys. "Yesterday I gave a man a blow job."

The frustrated janitor can't find blow jobs on the penance sheet. He asks, "What does Father usually give for a blow job?"

The altar boy replies, "Usually a Coke and a Milky Way."

Bill Clinton, Newt Gingrich, and Ross Perot are in a sinking boat. Who gets saved?

The American people.

Why does a man have a clear conscience?

Because he never uses it.

What does a man consider to be quality time with his wife?

Pulling the sheets over his head and saying, "Great chili, babe!"

What do you call an intelligent man in America?

A tourist.

———————

How is being at a singles bar different from going to the circus?

At the circus, the clowns don't talk.

———————

Why do black widow spiders eat their males after mating?

So they won't snore.

Why did Moses wander in the desert for forty years?

Because he wouldn't stop to ask for directions.

What's the difference between a new husband and a new dog?

After a year, a new dog is still excited to see you.

The night of the Halloween party, the couple were having trouble picking out costumes. The wife disappears into the kitchen and comes back a minute later, stark naked with only a lemon between her legs.

"And what are you supposed to be?" the husband wants to know.

"A sourpuss," the wife replies.

The husband then disappears into the kitchen and comes back with a potato hanging from his cock.

"And what are *you* supposed to be?" the wife asks.

The husband says, "If you're going as a sourpuss, I'm going as a dick-tater!"

A woman is pregnant with triplets. While she is waiting in line at a bank, two robbers come in and shoot the place up. The pregnant woman takes three bullets in the stomach.

She's rushed to the hospital and patched up. The doctor tells her that each baby has a bullet in it.

She asks the doctor, "Will my babies be okay?"

The doctor says, "Don't worry. The bullets will pass through their systems by way of normal metabolism."

The woman gives birth and has two girls and a boy. Fifteen years later, one of the girls says to her mother, "Mommy, I just passed a bullet into the toilet while I was going pee-pee."

Her mother tells her not to worry about it. A week later, her other daughter comes to her and says, "Mommy, I just passed a bullet in the toilet while I was going poo-poo."

The mother tells her not to worry about it. A week later, her son comes up to her and says, "Mommy, you're not gonna believe this but—"

"Don't tell me," the mother says. "You passed a bullet into the toilet, right?"

"Nope," the boy says. "I was jerking off and I shot the dog!"

What do you call an Italian slum?

A spaghetto.

_____

Why did the shit cross the road?

The chicken forgot to wipe its ass.

_____

What do you call a Polack with 500 girl-friends?

A shepherd.

What's the difference between a circumcision and a crucifixion?

With a crucifixion, you throw away the whole Jew.

———————

Two flies land on a big smelly turd and proceed to have lunch.
The first fly blows a huge fart.
The second fly says, "Do you mind? I'm trying to eat!"

———————

Why do farts smell?

So deaf people can enjoy them too.

What's the definition of "marriage"?

A very expensive way to get your laundry done.

———————

Why are men with pierced ears better prepared for marriage?

They've experienced pain and bought jewelry.

———————

Why is marriage like a three-ring circus?

1) Engagement ring
2) Wedding ring
3) Suffering

Why didn't the husband report his stolen credit card?

Because the thief was spending less than his wife did.

Why didn't the sanitary pads say hello to the Tampax?

Because the Tampax were stuck-up cunts.

A guy walks up to a woman who's wearing a fur coat.

He says to her and says, "Do you know how many animals had to die for that fur coat?"

She says to him, "Do you know how many animals I had to *fuck* for this coat?"

What do you call an Amish guy with his hand up a horse's ass?

A mechanic.

———————

What's the difference between a girl and a toilet?

A toilet doesn't want to cuddle after you drop a load into it.

Gross Gay and Lesbian Jokes

Why are gay guys never lonely?

They have friends up the ass.

———————

   "Daddy! Daddy! What's a homosexual?"
   "Shut up and suck my dick!"

What do a lawyer and a gay prostitute have in common?

They both make a living fucking people up the ass.

A guy gets thrown in jail. His cellmate is a hulking, six-foot-six black guy.

The black guy says, "You wanna be the husband or the wife?"

The other guy replies, "Uh, I guess I'll be the husband."

"Okay," the black dude says. "Get over here and suck your wife's dick."

How do you know when you're in a gay amusement park?

They pass out gerbils in the Tunnel of Love.

———————

Why did the doctors give the AIDS patient six more weeks to live?

A gerbil came out of his ass and saw his shadow.

———————

How did the fag burn his asshole?

He forgot to blow out the candle.

How do gay men like their eggs?

Up their asses.

———————

What was the lesbian's favorite flavor of ice cream?

Anchovy.

———————

What's the definition of "frenzy"?

Five dykes locked in a tuna fish factory.

Get Grossed Out
With More Jokes by Julius Alvin

Mickey Rawlings Mysteries
By Troy Soos

___**Hunting a Detroit Tiger**   **$5.99**US/**$7.50**CAN
    1-57566-291-4

___**Murder at Ebbets Field**   **$4.99**US/**$5.99**CAN
    1-57566-027-X

___**Murder at Fenway Park**   **$4.99**US/**$5.99**CAN
    0-8217-4909-9

___**Murder at Wrigley Field**   **$5.50**US/**$7.00**CAN
    1-57566-155-1